Halls Aflame

An Account of

The Spontaneous Revivals

At Asbury College in 1950 and 1958

by
Henry C. James
Paul Rader

Introduction by
Robert E. Coleman

First Fruits Press
Wilmore, Kentucky
c2013

ISBN: 9781621711025

Halls Aflame: An Account of the Spontaneous Revivals at Asbury College in 1950 and 1958, by Henry C. James and Paul Rader. Introduction by Robert E. Coleman.
First Fruits Press, © 2013
Asbury Seminary Press, © 1959

Digital version at
http://place.asburyseminary.edu/firstfruitsheritagematerial/66/

For all other uses, contact:

First Fruits Press
B.L. Fisher Library
Asbury Theological Seminary
204 N. Lexington Ave.
Wilmore, KY 40390
http://place.asburyseminary.edu/firstfruits

James, Henry C.
    Halls aflame : an account of the spontaneous revivals at Asbury College in 1950 and 1958 / by Henry C. James and Paul Rader ; introduction by Robert E. Coleman.
    Wilmore, Ky. : First Fruits Press, c2013.
    60 p. : ill., port. : 21 cm.
    Reprint. Previously published: Wilmore, Ky. : Asbury Seminary Press, c1959.
    ISBN: 9781621711025 (pbk.)
    1. Revivals – Kentucky – Wilmore. 2. Asbury College (Wilmore, Ky.)
    Subject. I. Title. II. Rader, Paul A. (Paul Alexander), 1934-
BV3775.W5 J35 2013   269.2

Cover design by Kelli Dierdorf

asburyseminary.edu
800.2ASBURY
204 North Lexington Avenue
Wilmore, Kentucky 40390

First Fruits
THE ACADEMIC OPEN PRESS OF ASBURY SEMINARY

HALLS AFLAME

An Account Of

THE SPONTANEOUS REVIVALS

At Asbury College in 1950 and 1958

by

Henry C. James

and

Paul Rader

Introduction by

Robert E. Coleman

1959

II Chronicles 7:14

"If my people which are called by my name, shall

humble themselves and pray, and seek my

face, and turn from their wicked

ways; then will I hear

from heaven, and will forgive

their sin, and will heal their land."

Acts 4:31

"And when they had prayed, the place was shaken

where they were assembled together; and

they were all filled with the

Holy Ghost, and they

spake the word

of God with

boldness."

i

INTRODUCTION

In a day when unprecedented numbers of people have a form of religion while at the same time the church seems unable to stem the rising tide of degeneracy that threatens the land, the question might be raised: Why this paradox? Should not the church have influence for righteousness in proportion to her numbers? However one may seek to answer this question, it is obvious that what we need is not more religion, but more power. In short, we need real revival!

For this reason, the account of the spontaneous revivals at Asbury College in 1950 and 1958 is very timely and provocative of thought. It shows what God can do when given a chance. The particular manifestations of these visitations of God may differ from others, for no two revivals are exactly alike. However, basic principles are reflected here which recur in all genuine spiritual awakenings. The sense of need, effectual prayer, confession and repentance, imparting of new life, infilling of the Holy Spirit and compulsion to tell the good news to others; these are relevant to every age.

The authors of these stories are well-qualified to speak, having experienced the events which they describe. Henry C. James, an alumnus, was himself converted during the revival of 1950; and Paul Rader, student leader on the Asbury campuses, was an active participant in the 1958 awakening. They are thus enabled through their close association with these revivals to transmit much of the moving drama of those days.

It is my hope that those who read these pages will catch something of the spirit which motivated its writing. But even more, I trust that many will be inspired to pray, to work and to believe God for revival today. The power of God is the same. The conditions for revival have not changed. We are the only variable factors in experiencing greater things than described in these pages. Trusting that this book will be used to open our eyes, I join the Psalmist in praying: "Wilt thou not revive us again; that thy people may rejoice in thee?" (Psalms 85:6).

Robert E. Coleman, Ph. D.
Sollie E. McCreless Professor of Evangelism
Asbury Theological Seminary

iii

PREFACE

There is a two-fold purpose for writing this booklet: namely that those interested may be able to read an account of these spontaneous revivals and that the knowledge of these might inspire and enrich the spiritual lives of the readers.

However, it would be attempting the impossible to put on paper all that took place from Thursday, February 23, at nine o'clock in the morning to Wednesday, March 1, 1950. As Dr. W. W. Holland, a faculty member at that time, expressed it: "No artist could paint the picture, no pen describe it, and it eludes the lens of the camera. The full conception of it must await the revelation of the Eternal Day."

The same might be said of the last revival at Asbury which began on March 1, at eight o'clock in the morning and ended March 4, 1958, with services each following night for the remainder of the week.

This book seeks only to sketch briefly the panorama of these events. The materials used for these stories has been obtained from newspaper articles, accounts given in the Pentecostal Herald, the Herald, the Asbury Collegian and various reports appearing in the press. Permission was granted to use material written and pictures taken by newsmen from the Courier-Journal, the Lexington Leader, and Dallas Morning News and the Lexington Herald.

This book first appeared in 1957 under the title, God's People Revived. The response to the first edition was so gratifying that at the suggestion of Dr. Robert E. Coleman it is being republished under the title, Halls Aflame. With the assistance of Mr. Paul Rader the entire booklet has been revised and the narrative passages rewritten. An effort has been made to eliminate repetition, and to include valuable materials not available at the time of the first edition. A brief account of the last spontaneous revival at Asbury College in 1958 has been added.

As this book is presented for publication, the authors join in earnest prayer that it will be attended by the blessing of God. May the Holy Spirit use the accounts of these pages to cause every reader to hunger and thirst after that righteousness that is obtainable only through a baptism with the cleansing flame of Pentecost.

MY PEOPLE

In the days when Kentucky stood on the edge of the western wilderness, Methodism's pioneer bishop, Francis Asbury, organized a small school for the training of Christian young people on the banks of the Kentucky River about three miles south of Wilmore. Founded in 1790, it was the oldest Methodist Church school in Kentucky. One hundred years later, in 1890, Dr. John Wesley Hughes began conducting college classes in a frame building at the tiny village of Wilmore in the heart of the Blue Grass region. Named for Bishop Asbury, "The Prophet of the Long Road," this institution was in a sense a successor of his pioneer academy.

Dr. Hughes, under the direction of the Holy Spirit, founded Asbury College to provide adequate academic training in a positively spiritual atmosphere. He wanted to send into the church and world a vital stream of Spirit-filled young men and women adequately equipped, intellectually and spiritually to confront the challenge of their day.

Today, the vision of the early founders of Asbury College has come to realization. The development of the physical plant from that first frame building still standing on Asbury's campus to a $2,000,000 plant housing over 900 students, is unusual, though not distinctive. It is the actualization of the spiritual vision of the organizers of the institution that is most striking. The impact of the school's alumni has been felt around the world. Asbury and Asburians have consistently been leaders in evangelism and missionary activity. In Methodism alone, there are more missionaries on the field today from Asbury College than from any other educational institution in the world.

Although Asbury was founded by a Methodist and its leadership as well as its student body has been through the years predominately Methodist, it is incorporated as an interdenominational institution, and is supported by a private constituency. Students come from about forty states and ten foreign countries representing some thirty denominations.

Approaching the front of Hughes Memorial Auditorium on the campus, one will see carved in the cornerstones these words: "Free salvation for all men and full salvation from all sin," and "Follow peace with all men and holiness without which no man shall see the

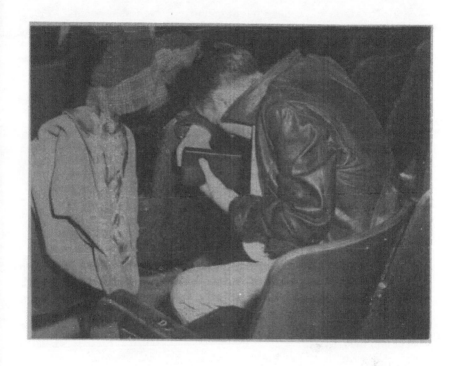

"People knelt alone in prayer everywhere in the auditorium; others sat quietly weeping or remained quiet as the Spirit dealt with them   ''

Lord. " (Hebrews 12:14). These inscriptions concisely represent the doctrinal foundation on which the school has stood since its founding. From its organization in 1890 it has adhered to and proclaimed the Wesleyan interpretation of the doctrine of Scriptural Holiness.

In view of such a heritage, it is not unusual that God has seen fit to bless this institution now and again through its history with mighty revivals which have been phenomenal in power and extent. However, in March of 1950, Asbury College experienced a visitation of God, the transforming impact of which will be felt in that institution until Jesus comes. The doctrinal statements chiseled in stone on the face of Hughes Memorial Auditorium were indelibly penned with a flame of fire on the hearts of those who experienced the mighty anointing of those days. It is to share the dynamic influence of that season of Heaven-sent revival that these pages are written.

February 23, 1950, on Thursday morning at the regular 9:00 a. m. chapel service, Rev. and Mrs. Dee Cobb, special guests for the hour, stood and sang:

"Let me lose myself and find it, Lord, in Thee.
May all self be slain, my friends see only Thee.
Though it cost me grief and pain, I will find my life again,
If I lose myself, I'll find it Lórd, in Thee. "

Rev. Cobb, now a Methodist pastor, said the Holy Spirit seemed to specially bless their hearts as they sang and to apply the truth of the song to those who listened. A holy hush settled down as he was to begin the message. At that moment Robert Barefoot stood for a word of praise for a prayer meeting which a group of boys had the night before where a number of them had found the Lord. Others rose to their feet for testimony, and this witnessing would have continued had not the leader of the service stepped forward to say he thought time should be given for the speaker to bring his message.

Sensing something unusual about the atmosphere of the hour, Rev. Cobb was somewhat reluctant to speak, but felt led of the Lord to read the Scripture and bring an abbreviated message on the text: "But I wholly followed the Lord my God. " (Joshua 14:8). The Spirit seemed to direct as he preached.

It was as though an electric shock moved over the whole place, and there was such a sense of the presence of God that one felt almost as though he could just reach out and touch Him. From where I stood I would probably best describe it as something like a gentle breeze sweeping across a broad field of wheat. Everyone seemed moved, tears started down some cheeks, and a rapture of delight stirred some to gentle laughter. All over the auditorium young people were standing. Then some, weeping, started to the altar. From then on it was like feasting on the heavenlies.[1]

From that moment God had charge of the meeting. Dr. W. W. Holland, Chairman of the Division of Philosophy and Religion at that time recalls:

> So mighty was the presence of the Holy Spirit in that chapel service that the students could not refrain from testimony. The guest speaker had little opportunity for his message. The flood-gates of heaven lifted and God moved into our midst as I have never before witnessed. The Holy Spirit fell upon the entire audience and everything broke loose. Testimonies were followed by confessions, confessions by crowded altars, crowded altars gave place to glorious spiritual victories, and this in turn to more testimonies. Thus, it ran for several days, wave after wave of glory swept the vast audiences; triumph after triumph took place at the altar. At times the Divine Presence was so pronounced that one could gather some conception of what Saint Paul must have experienced when he was caught up into the Third Heaven.[2]

He said the high point of that service was the confession period. This was such a sacred experience, when student after student laid bare his heart in confessing the wrongs done and asking forgiveness, that it seemed out of place to narrate it. This, however, deepened the conviction and students pled with fellow-students to confess and repent and find God. This proved to be the most effective kind of preaching, and the great altar, which overflowed to the row of chairs, was filled again and again. Indeed the tremendous altar services, the constant flow of testimonies over the public address system, and the ecstatic joy of the audience went on simultaneously; but it all blended into the harmony of a Heavenly symphony.

This service which started on Thursday at 9:00 o'clock in the morning continued uninterrupted throughout the day and into the night. There could be no dismissal, and long after midnight the crowd remained. The suggestion that the people go to their rest and return in the morning brought small response. About three hundred people remained all night in the chapel to pray.

At 6:00 o'clock Friday morning the services were still going on. Almost immediately thereafter the crowds began to assemble. They

9

seemed to have been drawn by a mighty magnet. Indeed they were for Christ was lifted and He drew them.

All day Friday the tide kept rising and a long line of students stood awaiting their turn to testify. For three days there was never a time when there were not people waiting in line to give their testimonies. Dr. Holland continues:

> I have seen the flood waters of rivers, and have read of breaking dams releasing almost unlimited reservoirs of water to augment the flood which was beyond its banks; so I can faintly visualize the lifting of the floodgates of Heaven releasing His immeasurable flood of grace and glory. Something tremendous struck the audience Friday night. Far into the morning, God was banking His glory mountain high!"[3]

Thus the services continued through Saturday, Sunday, Monday and Tuesday. The audience was advised to attend the various churches of Wilmore on Sunday morning. Most of the group did, but the spontaneous prayer chain at the college chapel was unbroken.

No service was announced for the following morning; in fact, none were announced from Thursday through Sunday. Sunday afternoon and night were tremendous services. They were still going full force at 2:00 o'clock Monday morning. Many people refused to leave the auditorium at all. The dean permitted the young men to remain, but the ladies went to their dormitories, where prayer services continued under the direction of their monitors.

On Tuesday morning, March 1, the last three worshippers left the auditorium at 7:00 a. m. , thus ending the around-the-clock prayer vigil and testimony services. However, throughout the remainder of the week, capacity crowds were on hand each night to hear Dr. T. M. Anderson and Dr. Z. T. Johnson exhort believers and instruct new converts in regular guidance and evangelistic services. During these meetings throughout the remainder of the revival hundreds of people sought the Lord. God was the leader of it all!

A Needy People

The revival level was the norm for the New Testament Church. But it is a plain fact of history that God's people have failed to consistently maintain the miracle level of such Christian living. Satan is an expert at insidiously draining the spiritual vitality of God's people.

But no sooner does sin begin to infiltrate the ranks of Christendom, than God finds those after His own heart who cry in desperation for a visitation of Divine power that will turn His people back to the old paths. David cried, "Wilt thou not revive us again, that thy people may rejoice in thee? (Psalms 85:6), and Habakkuk interceded in his generation, "O Lord, revive thy work in the midst of the years" (Habakkuk 3:2). Whenever declension, complacency and mediocrity chill the hearts of the saints, revival is God's program of recovery.

Asbury College has consistently placed strong emphasis on the spiritual disciplines and on high standards of conduct. One wonders why revival should be necessary at such a place. It is important to remember the admonition of the Word, "Keep thy heart with all diligence; for out of it are the issues of life" (Proverbs 4:23). When the Christian backslides, long before the standards of morality are lowered and the spiritual disciplines are abandoned, the hearts affection grows cool and its interests become worldly. Sins of disposition indicate a heart need that will issue in sins of commission - or, unholy deeds that will separate the soul from its source of life.

At the college, the great majority of students testified to having been born-again. But in the senior class there were some who, in spite of the intensive evangelistic emphasis, had never accepted Christ. Soon to leave the college, they were a special concern to those who were carrying a burden of prayer for the salvation of the student body.

Many more were at a stand-still in their Christian experience, failing to go on into the fulness of the Spirit. A dullness and stupor had invaded the lives of many Christians so that their testimonies were hindered and few souls, if any, sought God under their ministry. Don Gray writing for the college newspaper later reflected:

We here at Asbury had for sometime been shunning, be-

11

"Testimonies were followed by confessions, by crowded altars, glorious spiritual victories, and this in turn to more testimonies."

littling, and rebelling against the God that we so diligently serve. Our rebellion was not an open, declared warfare in most cases, but could more accurately be described as a silent, almost unwilling falling away from God. This process continued until many of us here were totally out of touch with God and yet professing to serve Him. There were students here bound by their sins and apparently satisfied to go ahead that way. Many who had trusted God for forgiveness of sins needed a purity and a power in their lives. [4]

Miss Lavetta Serrott, a member of the faculty, observed that there were many attitudes and feelings that were not befitting God's people. Not only was a great part of the student body at a low point spiritually, but general conduct was often not conducive to vital Christianity.

Long before indications of the declined spirituality were noticeable to the less sensitive, a great corps of God-owned students and faculty members who, by reason of their close walk in the Spirit possessed keen spiritual perception were desperately concerned at the sinking level of spiritual vitality. Immediately they began to pour out their hearts in passionate intercession for a mighty wave of Heaven-sent revival. They pleaded for penetrating conviction that would mortify spiritual pride, lay bare the festering sins of the flesh and spirit and break up the fallow ground of apathy, indifference, and fruitlessness. As always, God honored the persistent pleading of honest, hungry hearts. Revival came!

A Praying People

It is inevitable that many should inquire, "What is it that causes such spontaneous revival movements?" In the case of the Asbury awakening, there were several significant factors that combined to bring it about. One of these was the general spirit of revival which prevailed in many sections of the country. The Billy Graham Crusade in Los Angeles, California and the Wheaton College revival were contemporary with the unusual stirring of the Spirit at Asbury. However, in the minds of those who witnessed this awakening there remains little doubt that the most significant factor was fervent and prevailing prayer.

The Asbury institutions since their founding have always been the subject of earnest intercession on the part of God's saints around the world. As has been pointed out, shortly before this mighty outpouring of the Spirit, Christians in the town of Wilmore and elsewhere began to sense an increasing concern for the spiritual life of the school. Groups met to earnestly plead for a refreshing visitation of God.

It would be hard to point to any one person, or group of persons, and say that the revival came because of their praying alone. God honored the persistent prayers of persons whose names will never be connected with this movement. Many obscure Christians had poured out their souls to God in the secret of their rooms not only at Asbury, and in Wilmore, but in many parts of the world.

However, on Wednesday evening, at the request of an unsaved student, Herbert Van Vorce, several fellows met in the gymnasium to help him through to God. Also, there were others in the group who were subjects of prayer. The particulars of that prayer meeting and its result in "Herbie's" life will be discussed later. Suffice it to say, that when they parted about 3:00 a.m. this influential young man had found radiant victory in Christ, and the faith of the others for immediate revival was abounding. The next morning, when Robert Barefoot stood to testify in the chapel service he did so to share the overflow of that prayer meeting and report Herbie's victory. What followed is history.

Dr. W. Curry Mavis, professor of the Pastoral Relations Department at Asbury Theological Seminary recalls:

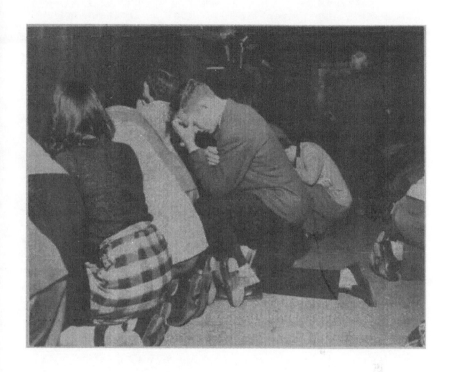

" Asbury has become an island of prayer . . . . "

For several weeks before the meeting started there had been much earnest prayer for an outpouring of the Spirit of God. Groups of students and faculty people met in the dormitory rooms and offices to pray. This spirit of prayer continued while the meeting was in progress. Frequently every room in the college auditorium building was occupied by groups of people in silent prayer. At other times, as the main service was in progress, the voices of prayer could be heard in other parts of the building. [5]

During the revival there were prayer meetings in progress everywhere, in the dormitories, in the classrooms, in the dining hall, in the gymnasium, on the campus, and in the homes of Wilmore residents. A spirit of prayer seemed to possess each person that had attended the services and felt the presence of God. It was common to hear the praying of Christians from almost any point of the campus. They offered petitions first for themselves that they might be used of God without hindrance and then that sinners might be saved through their witness.

The people whose lives were revitalized were now in a condition to pray for the lost, not only for people in Wilmore, but in the surrounding towns and communities. · It was not until then that students could really pray for their classmates. Fellow-students who were not saved recognized the difference in the lives of their Christian friends, who became a definite witness.

The spirit of prayer was compelling in its appeal. One student, Ruby Vahey recounted that:

Shortly after dawn Friday morning several hundred students returned to the auditorium and knelt and prayed. It was 'World Day of Prayer' and their requests encompassed the globe. Classes were resumed at eight o'clock, but those who were free at that hour found it impossible to tear themselves away from the sacred spot. Teachers and students were unable to bring themselves back so suddenly from the heavenly to the earthly, and every class that morning was transformed into a prayer or praise meeting. [6]

Even the newsmen were deeply impressed with the volume of prayer. The Dallas Morning News stated; "A religious revival that has made Asbury College an island of prayer is attracting persons from other Kentucky cities to this small town. There was no indication early this morning as to when the prayers and testimonials would end."

Jack Lewyn, reporter for the Lexington Herald recorded the following statement concerning the spirit of prayer:

Prayer, and little else, dominated life in this little Jessamine-County college tonight.
Voices toned with sincerity and eyes sparkling with a dampness of inner realization were uplifted to God as a thousand revival participants prayed and rendered testimonies with undiminishing dedication.
A general revival session in Hughes Memorial Auditorium on the Asbury College campus was suspended temporarily shortly after noon, but as an overcast sky faded into night-fall, the 1,200-capacity chapel, almost large enough to accomodate the town's population, echoed again with declarations of faith.
The suspension followed a morning-long series of faculty testimonies and prayers, but the revival has never been interrupted since it began at 9:00 a.m. Thursday, when a student stood and asked to make a testimony.
Although the chapel was closed for an hour, groups of fifty or more students and townspeople continued to pray and 'find God' in meetings in dormitories, homes and other campus chapels.
Shortly after Hughes Auditorium was reopened, the participants began returning in small groups to pray, confess, and testify perhaps throughout the night amid patient, impressive meditation.
Despite the shouts, the declarations, individual and grouped, an air of meditation prevailed as students, older folks and children knelt with heads bowed and eyes damp. Many never shouted, but prayed silently with a depth of feeling.
When the hymns resounded, the singing became almost thunderous.... This service rolled on through the night with some sixty students remaining in the auditorium kneeling in prayer. Others returned to dormitories to get some rest, but many, instead of sleeping, held prayer meetings in rooms. [8]

The testimony of history is that at the heart of every genuine spiritual awakening there is a revival of prevailing intercession. Thus it was in the Asbury refreshing. Prayer was the secret of the power and presence of God. When people call upon the Lord in humility and sincerity, they may with confidence expect that He will lay bare His mighty arm and visit with blessing on His people.

Conviction seemed to leap from heart to heart and soon the Spirit of prayer was registered on the hearts as well as the faces of those who had come into contact with the living God!

A Spirit-filled People

The first powerful impact of the Spirit, that eventful Thursday morning brought searching, soul-searing, conviction on the hearts of those outside of Christ. Sin was made real and black. God and His claims were inescapable. Students began to bring forth fruits meet for repentance.

From the time of the first response during the chapel hour, the altar was seldom if ever empty until the initial continuous stage of the revival ended on Tuesday. Hundreds of Asbury students were born again of the Spirit. Others, living below their privileges in Christ sought the Baptism with the Holy Ghost. Backsliders felt the press of the Spirit compelling them to return to former victory.

As the movement gained attention through nationwide newspaper and television coverage, visitors and friends began to come to the campus out of curiosity. Many of these who came to the auditorium indifferently were immediately clutched by the conviction of the Spirit, and before long, making their way down the aisle, they took their place amidst the scores of others earnestly seeking forgiveness and cleansing at the altar of prayer.

One such person was Mr. Jimmy Rose of Paris, Kentucky. At that time, Mr. Rose was coaching a state championship basketball team at the Paris High School. The following tells of his experience:

In late February 1950 I recall as a young basketball coach I was finishing my seventh year as a mentor here in Kentucky. I was beginning to feel the tremendous pressure that most coaches feel here in this state as the tournaments are about to roll around. The year before my team at Paris had finished fourth in the state and I felt the community would not be happy with my services if I did any less that year. Only a coach in similar circumstances can fully appreciate the mental torture of those close games that determine one's future in the coaching profession.

Two years before, a referee who was a ministerial student at Asbury College had witnessed to me in the lobby of the Phoenix Hotel in Lexington, Kentucky, following a game we had played against Inez High School. This young man, Ford

"For three days there was never a time when there were not people waiting in line to give testimonies."

Philpot, now one of the most successful evangelists in the Methodist Church, told me what Christ had done for him. He told me that he had a peace that nothing in this world could possibly give. One could sense by his countenance and conversation that he had truly found the peace he was talking about. I left him that day knowing that he had something I desperately needed.

When I read in the papers about the spontaneous revival going on at the college, I remembered the conversation with Ford Philpot. I was curious to know about the experience to which he witnessed. The Rev. Earl Curry accompanied me to Wilmore.

My most vivid memory of that day was when I opened the door of Hughes Auditorium. Although I could not explain it then, I know now that it was the presence of the Holy Spirit. Others have testified to having felt this supernatural presence upon entering the building. There was a certain feeling about His presence that gave one a sense of peace and surrender. I have felt the presence of the Holy Spirit on many occasions since then, but never in such power.

I remember taking a seat with Rev. Curry about half way down on the left side. Several students were kneeling at the altar, and a young man by the name of Bob Barefoot was on the platform exhorting. Afterwards a series of young people came to the platform and gave their testimonies. Many told of the calls they had received during the meeting to go to foreign mission fields. Many said they had found the Lord for the first time, while others spoke of spiritual victories in their homes where mothers, fathers, brothers, and sisters had been converted during the last forty-eight hours. One could tell these testimonies were real and convincing.

I was so impressed and so moved by the Holy Spirit that I could not fight any longer the call of God for my life. I made my way to the altar and very quietly but sincerely surrendered my life to Him. I received the peace that day that Ford Philpot had spoken to me about two years before. I later went to the platform and gave my testimony, which went something like this: 'My name is Jimmy Rose and I am a basketball coach at Paris High School here in Kentucky. I want each of you to know that the Lord has saved me and called me into full-time Christian service. If He will let me live until next September I will give up my coaching and enroll at Asbury Seminary.' Through His grace I am now an ordained minister of the Methodist Church.

Dr. Holland recounts some incidents illustrative of the power of the Spirit during these hours:

Sunday night two young men came from the Baptist college at Campbellsville, Kentucky. They were so blessed that they drove home seventy miles after service and brought back between twenty and thirty of their fellow-students, arriving at Wilmore at four o'clock Monday morning, while the service of prayer and praise was still on. The students felt the need of help, and sent for Dr. T. M. Anderson, a faculty member to come to their aid. He came, preached to them for thirty minutes and had an altar call; with the result that many were blessed. They left at five-thirty o'clock, in time to get home for school; but they returned on Monday evening with a larger delegation.

A Freshman was wonderfully sanctified. He felt he must tell his mother and help her into the Christian experience. He secured an auto and drove two hundred miles to his home in Tennessee. He told the good news to his mother and brought her back with him in time for her to be gloriously saved in the service that evening.

A Salvation Army captain from Middletown, Ohio, on his way to a weekend engagement turned on his radio and got the news report of the revival. He turned in this direction. After filling his engagement on Sunday, he was back again on Monday. We made no complete record of visitors, but we know people came from Michigan, Illinois, Indiana, Ohio, Tennessee, West Virginia, Florida, Mississippi, Georgia, and from all over Kentucky.

After a spontaneous desire to call her home at Brookhaven, Mississippi, a student asked her two unsaved brothers to come for the revival. One brother was a soldier who was home on furlough after having just returned from Okinawa. Both accepted their sister's invitation, and, with their mother, drove a distance of seven hundred miles, arriving at Asbury at 8:30 p.m. Sunday evening. Shortly after entering Hughes Auditorium, they responded to the exhortation given by Dr. T. M. Anderson, and made their way to the already-filled altar, where they were gloriously saved. The following evening one of the brothers felt his need for the baptism of the Holy Spirit and was sanctified. The Christian mother rejoiced exceedingly over the two victories for which she had been praying for years. The members of the family group were thankful that they had driven such a great distance to share in the blessings of the revival.[9]

One of the most convincing indications of the genuineness of the revival was a spirit of complete honesty with God and man. Students were evidently broken and humiliated under the burden of their sin. Many stood and publicly sought forgiveness for wrongs done, ill-feelings, and un-Christian conversation. Scores of others privately settled differences with offended persons. Many of these who prayed and found peace, went to fellow-students and made restitution for wrongs. Those to whom the restitutions were made began to investigate their own spiritual lives. Brokenness, contrition, honest repentance and restitution typified the spirit of penitents.

Throughout these hours of heart-searching conviction hundreds of Christians were convinced of their need for heart cleansing and the baptism with the Holy Ghost. Influential spiritual leaders among the students became aware of fruitlessness, fear of man, pride, and other sins of the spirit that were robbing them of victory. They hungered and thirsted after righteousness, and in response to a dying to all self and faith in the cleansing power of the blood they were filled with the purifying, empowering presence of the Holy Spirit. As these students were wholly sanctified, they became instruments of blessing. They witnessed and prayed, exhorted and counseled, seeking out the lost and bringing them to the Saviour. Heart purity brought not only power in witnessing, but an unquenchable passion to do so. Hundreds were personally confronted with the claims of Christ and the revival continued to pyramid in power and blessing.

One unique aspect of the revival was an unusual gift of spiritual discernment given to Dr. T. M. Anderson. The following incident gives indication of the unusual manifestations of the Spirit's power that were experienced at the time.

There was a young woman who was unmoved by the power of God during the revival. She told some of the students that it was nothing but emotionalism and excitement and that she would have nothing to do with it. Several students requested that Dr. Anderson join them in prayer for the girl to be saved. About four o'clock in the morning he began to pray for this girl. He did not know her but the moment he began to pray, he saw her running out of a lighted building into the darkness. The vision so impressed him that he told some of the students to inform the young woman that he had seen her running from God.

About nine thirty o'clock that night, the girl went to Dr. Anderson's home and in anger told him that she wanted no part of the revival, that it was all emotionalism and religious excitement. He could not reason with her for she was very angry at him for sending word to her about running from God.

Dr. Anderson relates the story this way:

In my own mind, I was convinced that her attitude toward the revival was a pretense and that her real reason was covering her sins. I told her I could find the real reason for rejecting the Saviour, and I began to pray for her. When I presented her before the Saviour, I saw a large hall, and an orchestra and the leader of the orchestra standing before a microphone. But my attention was drawn to a young man playing the piano. I knew he had something to do with this girl's attitude toward Christ. When I asked the girl about the young man, she began to cry and confessed that she had been attending the dance and at one time planning to marry the piano player. She said it was a secret and was amazed that I knew it.

As I began to pray again for her, I saw a lighted room and a table set; and this young woman filling the glasses with liqour. When I asked her if she drank liqour, she began to scream and said, 'That is a cocktail party given in my home, and I gave a preacher's daughter her first drink. I have damned her; I have damned my best friend!' She confessed covering her many evil deeds by pretending that she did not believe in the revival. She had no more rebellion left in her; she was completely broken in spirit and was contrite of heart. Once more I took her to the Saviour in prayer and obtained mercy for her at the throne of grace. The merciful Lord saved her instantly; and she shouted with great joy for deliverance from sin. [10]

V

A Witnessing People

No sooner did the fire of God fall on the hearts of earnest seekers than they were empowered to spread the holy flame. What can be so contagious as pure hearts aflame with holy love? It was impossible to contain the glorious news. By simple, sincere, witness the revival spread through the college, the seminary, out into the town, throughout the state and across the country. As the word spread, visitors began to arrive from everywhere. Many were born again or baptised with the Spirit. Returning home, they would carry with them a white-hot revival in their hearts. Revivals spread wherever they went. Churches were set aflame, families were converted, and scores were brought to faith in Christ who had never been in Wilmore. The total effect of the outreach of the revival will not be known until the Lord returns. Only a few examples can be given to illustrate how God multiplied the fruits of this awakening.

The Asbury Collegian reported:

At 2:00 a. m. Monday, a call was received from a student at Kentucky Wesleyan College, who asked whether the revival was continuing. Several students arrived later that morning from the college to receive inspiration from the services, and they returned with a desire to share the revival spirit with their fellow-students.

During Sunday night's service a group of twenty-five local high school students came forward to testify of God's saving grace. Two Wilmore High School girls said they hoped to start a prayer meeting in their school on Monday during the lunch hour.

A seventeen-year-old high school student said he had come from his home in Irving, Kentucky, about fifty miles away. He stated that he had received a real experience and wanted to take it home to his school and community. A Lexington high school student also testified that he had a desire to take the spirit of the revival home and share it with others.

A student from the Southern Baptist Theological Seminary, Louisville, Kentucky, said with deepest sincerity, 'My prayer is that I may carry back with me something just like this, along with the power that is here.'

"These testimonies were radiant, natural, and definite . . . . "

A youth group from the Calvary Holiness Church arrived on campus Saturday for the revival service. One grade school student who was present, witnessed in his church on the following day and requested prayer for his schoolmates.[11]

At the time of the revival, Wayne Patton, now an evangelist of the Methodist Church, was youth director at the Hiland Methodist Church in Fort Thomas, Kentucky. He called from Asbury asking his parents to tell the young people that a wonderful revival had broken out at the college and to invite them to come down if they could.

Two young men, Don Walsh and Bill Parker, who had been saved in a weekend revival that was held by Wayne and Bob Scott at Fort Thomas came to the college and both through the ministry of Dr. T. M. Anderson were sanctified wholly.

They went back to northern Kentucky and a few days after that were in a sub-district meeting in one of the churches in that area. The Lord so mightily moved on the group through the testimonies of these young men that the minister in charge felt compelled to give an altar call at once. About forty young people responded. There was such joy among the converts that the leaders thought they ought to do something to keep the fires burning. So they began Saturday night evangelistic services under the name of The Christian Youth of Northern Kentucky. Hundreds of teen-agers sought the Saviour through the witness of these Saturday night rallies. Young people were attracted from fifteen or twenty miles away. This organization continued for four years and many revivals, prayer meetings, and Bible studies were sponsored by this group of young people. The impact was felt all over northern Kentucky. Several teen-agers won to Christ through its influence are now in the ministry.

Simple and bold testimony was the God-blessed method of spreading the movement. A student riding south on a bus fell into conversation with a preacher just behind the driver. The bus driver, hearing what they said about the Asbury revival, became so convicted that he requested permission of the passengers to pull to the side of the road for a period of prayer.

As the revival progressed, students began to receive invitations to come and witness to what God was doing at Asbury. Many students returning home for the weekend were given opportunities to report God's blessings in their home churches. Student pastors sensed the powerful anointing of God on their preaching, and great were the results.

The Collegian reported the results of the first weekend. Here is a portion of that report.

God blessed Ford Philpot's messages with twenty seekers at Mt. Carmel Church, Saturday evening, and there were approximately thirty seekers at Epworth Methodist Church in Lexington, Kentucky, on Sunday evening.

After testimonies began at Little Texas Mission, the planned sermon had to be put aside. In both the morning and evening services souls found satisfaction in their Lord Jesus.

Hearts melted and tears flowed freely down the cheeks of many at Ludlow Methodist Church in Ludlow, Kentucky, as God blessed the testimonies and songs of five students from Asbury. There were five victories plus many requests for prayer.

Earl Bishop, student, and his group held services in saloons as well as in the church. Hearts were touched and as always truth was victorious.

Twelve at Fort Valley, Georgia, found God after listening to the testimonies and prayers of another group of Asburians.

Fifteen young people knelt at the altar in Corbin, Kentucky, searching for soul satisfaction. George Rose and Phil Peace, under the direction of our Lord, were in charge.

Jesus visited the prison at Frankfort, Kentucky, and freed two souls.

At the Salvation Army Post in Danville, Kentucky, nine persons joined the forces of truth.

Janie Kunkel, Marilyn Loy, and Beverly Sund were thrilled to the depths of their souls when they saw God's Holy Spirit move the hearts of the people in the churches of Lanesville, Indiana and New Middletown, Indiana. Shouts and sobs were heard and heart wringings were felt as testimonies were given. It had been a long time since such emotions were displayed in these churches. [12]

One student felt the urge to drive to Mt. Carmel, Kentucky some ninety miles from Wilmore, and he held a meeting while there. He returned on Monday morning and reported twenty-two persons wonderfully sanctified in the meeting.

Rev. R. E. Case, pastor of the Wells Memorial Methodist Church in Jackson, Mississippi, at this time, called long distance requesting that a gospel team be sent to help him in a revival. A concerned Christian lady paid their transportation by air, and three students from Asbury College and one from Asbury Theological Seminary were on their way within a short time. They phoned back the next day, stating that the church was packed and people were standing in the streets, and between fifty and sixty people were at the altar. The next day they were invited to move to the largest tabernacle in the city of Jackson, with all the facilities at their command.

Here is the story of that meeting.as related by the pastor:

Four students came by plane from Asbury College to give a report on the great outpouring of the Holy Spirit there. Two of the students who came in that group were members of our church. We had a few spot announcements on the radio that the students were coming. They arrived late Wednesday afternoon by plane and came directly to the church. I was impressed by the holy hush and quietness that seemed to exist among these four students. They went into a room in the rear of the church for a period of prayer. I went out into the foyer of the church to greet the people who were beginning to arrive. This same holy hush seemed to prevail as the people gathered into the sanctuary. No one talked above a whisper. Some of our people went to the altar and prayed silently.

The service began at 7:30 p.m. It consisted of singing, testifying, and exhortation. Each member of the group told about the revival at Asbury and of the tremendous blessing he had received. Each one of them closed his testimony with a plea for the people of the audience to receive Christ as their Saviour and Sanctifier. The altar was filled twice that evening. The power of God was felt mightily. It was around ten o'clock, as I remember, when the service was over. We announced a service on the following night.

Thursday and Friday nights were almost duplicates of Wednesday night, except that the people of the congregation joined in the testimonies. God was present, and His power could be felt in an unusual way. On Saturday, Dr. T. M. Anderson arrived by plane with four more Asbury students. Saturday night was a high spot in the revival for us all. There were perhaps a dozen preachers on the rostrum. Dr. Anderson was the master of ceremonies, but at times one of the young preachers was in charge. "Amazing Grace" was sung in the spirit, and tears flowed while shouts of praise went up.

Preachers embraced each other on the rostrum, and the people wept. Dr. Anderson brought a message, and the altar was lined with seekers.

More Asbury boys came, some went to Hattiesburg, Mississippi, to the Broadstreet Church of which Rev. Andrew Gallman was pastor, and a revival broke out there. Another group started a revival at Natchez, Mississippi. Everything was informal. Speakers spoke extemporaneously. Men would come down the aisle and upon the rostrum to testify and exhort.

The boys from Asbury, as well as Dr. Anderson, stressed the fulness of the Spirit. Visitors, who had never heard the doctrine preached, were impressed, and before long they were at the altar seeking the experience.

I remember one lady who came. She had a very pleasant personality, and the people were deeply impressed with her testimony. No one could doubt that she was a saved person. One night as we were leaving the church, this lady said to me, 'Brother Case, this is wonderful. I know that I am saved, but I do not have what these young men are preaching, the Baptism with the Holy Spirit. Do you have any books that you could let me read on the doctrine?' I assured her that I did, and that I would bring them to her the next night. This lady told me a couple of nights later that she was 'simply revelling in these books,' especially Wood's Perfect Love. She was sanctified in her home. She called us and told us about it. She was weeping over the phone. I gave her a special opportunity to testify to the experience before the whole congregation.

People came to the revival from six states. Of course, we could not accommodate the crowds. We had all night prayer meetings. Services lasted as late as two and three o'clock in the morning. It was a time of refreshing from the Lord. A noteworthy fact about this revival was the absence of denominational lines. The Holy Spirit prevailed and a spirit of love was there. Each service saw the sanctuary filled to overflowing. God was there! Prayer went up almost constantly. We experienced a foretaste of heaven.

I have found people from time to time who were saved in that revival. It seemed that more people outside of our church were blessed in a definite manner than were those of our membership. It was truly a wonderful visitation of God among us. We thank Him for permitting us to have this experience. [13]

It has been conservatively estimated that over four thousand persons received definite victory as a result of the revival at the college, through the witness of individuals and groups going from Wilmore to testify to God's unbounded blessing. Only the Lamb's Book of Life accurately recorded the precious fruit of that time of gracious refreshing from the presence of the Lord.

"It was a marvelous sight to see hundreds of hands spontaneously

raised in personal affirmation as the great hymns of the church were sung."

VI

TRANSFORMED PERSONS

There is no more convincing evidence of the truth of the Gospel than the witness of Christian experience. The skeptics and critics must finally confront the unanswerable apolegetic of transformed lives.

To appreciate the impact of the Asbury revival, one must think, not in terms of general blessing to all, but in terms of individuals made anew by the transforming touch of the Spirit of God. Words will never capture the thrill of hearing students, fresh from a regenerating encounter with the Lord Jesus, witness to the power and grace of God. From the hundreds of testimonies that might be given, an account of how three persons were affected by the personal impact of the revival is related.

Robert Barefoot was used of God during the revival as much as any other individual. Not only did he work and pray with those at the altar, but he dealt with the souls of those who lived in town. He would visit lost sinners and eventually win them to Christ. He was fearless in this type of work. His testimony that eventful morning in chapel sparked the revival which was to touch the ends of the earth. Many prayer groups received their inspiration because of the prayer life of this one student. His testimony given in the Collegian points up the power of his prayer life.

> Since I have been in Asbury College, the Devil has tried to tell me many times, 'Give up, Bob. There's no use to keep on praying. There is no use to keep on believing holiness.' In the first place I had a hard time getting into Asbury; sickness, discouragement, and everything else tried to get me to give up; but I held on in prayer and leaned on the everlasting arms of Jesus. Since this revival, I have found out that it pays to serve Jesus and keep true to Him, for He is in the prayer answering business and He will never fail. I praise Him for about forty-five answers to prayer. I believe this revival came because a group of us got together and prayed it down. [14]

On August 23 and 24, 1956, Robert and his wife, Louise were taken home to heaven as a result of an auto-truck collision near

Robert N. Barefoot

Herbert Van Vorce

Marshall, North Carolina, where they were on their way home from attending a meeting nearby.

Following the accident, Bob regained consciousness sufficiently at the hospital to recognize his district superintendent, Dr. J. W. Fitzgerald, and to quote one Psalm after another, particularly Psalms 23 and 121. Just before he passed away, Bob spelled out the word H-E-A-V-E-N and said, "It is beautiful! I wish Louise were here." His last request was granted and she joined him in the Church Triumphant the following day.

Bob Barefoot led many souls to Christ before his death. He had a burning passion for those that were lost and he used his dynamic personality to glorify the Christ he served. He was there the night that one of the authors of this book, Henry C. James was converted. Here, are the events leading to his encounter with God as he relates them.

I knew Bob Barefoot well, for in 1947 he had led my brother Clarence, who was as alcoholic, to God. I shall never forget the night I knelt at the altar and prayed through to complete victory in Christ. I can still see Bob's shining face raised heavenward shouting the praises of God.

I was employed at the city post office and when I saw the newspaper stories and heard about what was taking place at the college, I had to see it to believe it.

On Saturday night, I made my way to Hughes Auditorium curious to see what was happening. Previous to this, I rarely went to church. However, as I entered the building and reached the top of the balcony stairs, I had the most unusual feeling as I sensed a drawing power that swept over my whole being. It was hard to explain at that time, but now I realize it was the Holy Spirit present in great power. This was the most positive witness to me that this revival was not of human origin.

After the midnight hour the Lord met my need and forgave my many sins. Then followed another soul struggle about the call to preach the Gospel. This was the last thing that I desired to do. However, two days later I gave Him my life to be used as He pleased. The Holy Spirit filled my heart with joy and peace, taking the place of turmoil and strife. I am happy to be a witness for God and to preach the unsearchable riches of Christ.

When Herbert Van Vorce came to Asbury College he brought with him an impressive record as an athlete in high school, having been offered a scholarship to one of the leading colleges of this country.

Tall, well-built, he was handsome and personable. It wasn't long before he was as popular as any other boy on campus. But in spite of the fact that his father, Major H. J. Van Vorce, Army Chaplain and a man of God, gave him a strong Christian background, "Herbie" was skeptical of Christian truth. Before long his name headed many a godly students list of most wanted men for Christ.

The night before the revival started, he was trying to study in his room at Morrison Cottage, but conviction became so great that study was impossible. He left his work, went downstairs, awakened a fellow-student whom he asked to pray with him. The two boys went to a car and had a season of prayer, but Herbie could not seem to pray through. He suggested getting Bob Barefoot, whom he knew had been praying for months that he would make a full surrender to Christ. As they neared the dormitory, they met Bob and he told them he was coming to hunt Herbie, because God had told him Herbie needed help.

So the boys went to the old gymnasium and prayed until almost three in the morning, when the fire fell. In telling of this experience, Herbie said that when the Holy Spirit came, he felt as though dead and lay on the floor for some time before being able to leave.

Immediately, Herbie began to witness to his new-found faith. Everywhere he found opportunities to challenge others with what Christ could do in their lives. Herbie wrote his parents soon after he was converted and told of what God was doing:

It is Sunday again; I can truly say it has been one of the best Sundays of my life. Dwight Mikkelson and I with a few others went to Nicholasville to the jail and had a service and then went to Lexington and had a street meeting. We saw a man about fifty years of age gloriously saved. We went down in the slums for the service. However, the man that was saved was a middle class man whom we met uptown and had given a tract.

....after talking a while, he said he would like to become a Christian. We went over to the car and the man was gloriously saved.

Without doubt you have already sensed a change in my life. The other morning at three o'clock in the gym I settled it all with God. I started praying at twelve and at about three o'clock the fire fell. I put everything on the altar; Lois, my life ambition, everything. I don't know, but God has been revealing sermon after sermon to me. It wouldn't surprise me if He had the ministry in mind for me. I am going ahead and continue trying to get into Med. school, trusting that God's will

35

will be worked out. I can say I have never had such a glorious revelation of the Holy Spirit as I had the other night. God has been so gracious to me by giving me Christian parents who will take their stand for Jesus Christ and the fulness of His Spirit.

I haven't had a good night's sleep for two weeks until last night. Every night there would be a text running through my mind. I don't feel like a radical or that I am emotionally upset. I know what I want and settled it with God for time and eternity.

Well, folks, I love you and I felt I should let you know about my change and complete submission to God. Pray for me; I know you do without my asking.

The next letter was written about two or three days later:

How I wish you were here; it is wonderful what the Lord is doing. I have such peace and joy I can't express it. I can't write much because I have been in Heaven for three days, eaten three meals, had about three blessings, and walked about three hundred miles telling people that Jesus saves. I have asked I don't know how many merchants in town to come and get right with God. It is an outpouring of the Spirit. People are coming from all over, trying to figure it out and can't conceive of people shouting, getting to God. I am glad I didn't wait for this to make my decision for Christ. I have victory like I never had before. God has laid His hand on me. I am burning up for Jesus; Praise His Name! Dad, I have got what you got; I have it to stay. I am intoxicated with the Spirit; I can hardly write; my body feels like it is floating in heaven. I have caught hold of the hem of His garment. I am on the Gospel train that will stop at Hallelujah Station. I know you think I am going or gone crazy but God has so wonderfully got hold of me.

Reporters have been here from all over; you probably have heard about it. It (the revival) is now headed for the seventieth hour without stopping.

Between the second and third letters Herbie and some others had been in Mississippi holding meetings. The third letter was written at Wilmore. He tells about the revival which began in Jackson at the Wells Memorial Methodist Church:

God has marvellously helped me with my work; I am all caught up, ready to start studying for finals next week. If it is God's will, I am going back to Mississippi. Dr. (T. M.) Anderson spoke in the capitol building. We have no definite reports as yet on that service.

The Lord has so wonderfully blessed me I could never write in ink or explain in words what has been happening. I am going to the Church of the Open Door Sunday in Louisville, (Kentucky). Pray much for this service. Then I have an invitation to go to North Carolina in the First Methodist Church in Durham for a week's meeting and a week-end meeting in Fort Valley, Georgia. I am anxious to see souls saved.

The revival in Mississippi is spreading throughout the state; we are getting calls in fifteen or twenty towns wanting some one to come for city-wide meetings. Oh, the power of God and how He can use us when we completely forget self and plunge in with God.

It all seems like a dream; I have been singing and testifying in hugh churches and over radio stations that cover nine states - potentially thirty million people. It is unbelievable what God has done for me.

Herbie was the first victory of the revival - a babe in Christ, yet his witness had an immediate effectiveness that many a mature minister could not claim. For the next year and a half Herbie continued to grow in grace. God used him mightily in bringing young people to Christ.

Herbie was killed instantly by an electric shock on August 25, 1951, in Findlay, Ohio, while engaged in construction work. One of his last messages to his family was: "If you ever get a telegram saying I have gone unexpectedly, don't worry. I will be WITH JESUS!" It is estimated that several hundred persons found Christ during a brief year and a half as a result of Herbie's testimony in meetings in which he assisted in Mississippi, Texas, New York, and Kentucky. Now he has been called to a higher ministry.

At the funeral service, in Wilmore, Herbie's father, Chaplain H. J. Van Vorce, asked to give his son's testimony. Vividly he recalled events leading up to Herbie's remarkable conversion, preceding Asbury's spontaneous revival. Herbie phoned his folks, then in Texas: "Dad, I have good news for you and Mom. At three o'clock this morning in the old gym I said: 'Lord, you can have my life, my all, for the ministry or the mission field or whatever you want.'" A week later he phoned again: "Dad, you must come to Wilmore! The greatest revival I have ever seen is here. I did not know it could be so wonderful.   We have left this world and have gone to another."

As he stood beside the casket where lay the body of his son, Chaplain Van Vorce closed his remarks by saying: "I do not question the love of God.   I am going back to camp with new determination to preach the love of God and His power to sustain through the darkest hours!....God's will is our will.   My hope and prayer is that the mantle of this life might fall on some other boy or boys that they may go forth to do even greater things than Herbie could have done."

VII

PATTERNS AND PROBLEMS

The Asbury revival was not planned in advance by any human agency. It was from the beginning a movement directed by the Spirit of God. Preachers and preaching were not in prominence. God led, the people obeyed, and great were the results. It was glorious to see the leadership of the Spirit. Spontaneous witnessing characterized the meetings. This was not a preaching meeting as have been most of the revivals during the Twentieth Century. No sermon was delivered until the evening of the fourth day, and then they were more earnest exhortations than sermons.

Hundreds of people, most of them young, gave testimonies of having been saved, sanctified, or having received some other definite spiritual victory. These testimonies were radiant, natural, and definite, and stereotyped testimonies were the exception. The public 'confession' element was at a minimum though many private confessions and restitutions were made. The writer heard scores of testimonies and not one contained objectional elements. The press reporters who visited this meeting were deeply impressed with the reports of victory. Some of them quietly walked about as if they were on holy ground. After one college girl had witnessed to her personal commitment to God, one reporter, evidently unaccustomed to personal witnessing, stated that it seemed an intrusion to be present. [15]

Reporter Jack Lewyn of the Lexington Herald-Leader, published this account of the witnessing.

A co-ed at the interdenominational school, walked to a rostrum on the chapel stage and shouted: 'Praise the Lord.... because He met my need.... I've never felt like this before; I never knew the glory of Christ.'
During each pronunciation, shouts of 'Hallelujah' rang throughout the auditorium, affirming convictions.
Many confessed having found fault with their brethren and asked forgiveness. Others spoke firmly of their faith in God

the Almighty.

During tonight's service, one man stood and testified: 'I said I've been a Christian for nine years. I've been lying to you.' He said he had not, until now, been complete in his faith.

Dr. C. B. Hamann, a college professor, said he would like to see the old Methodist tradition of class meetings adopted. He asked two men, one elderly and one middle-aged, to testify to their experiences, and they did.

A wave of testimonies subsided, then rose again after a period of quiet reverent meditation.

Later Lewyn reported:

Townspeople and faculty members stood a little in awe of what Dean J. B. Kenyon called 'a sincere demonstration of faith,' as hundreds of students lined up to 'testify for God.' A blind student said he hoped 'the revival would spread to the state university at Lexington.'

Each student who was to speak walked to the front of a velvet curtain drawn before a stage set for the play, 'Our Hearts Were Young and Gay.' The play, scheduled to be given Friday night and tonight by the Junior Class, was postponed indefinitely.

Another student, an ex-member of the German Army and former prisoner of war in this country, said, 'It certainly is strange that I, a German who fought against the Americans, could come to a school like Asbury and make so many hundreds of friends. It all goes to show that God is everywhere.' He added, 'The only way for unity is through God.'

Men and women students alike wept openly as their classmates unburdened themselves, told how troubled their hearts had been and how happy they were to have confessed their faith openly.

'My heart was sad until I met Jesus,' one girl said. A Korean student, full of emotion, but at a loss for words, said, 'My tongue will not work but I have a big heart.'

Several students told the audience of some 1,200 that their parents were still living in sin. About a dozen said they had come to the predominately religious school more or less over the objections of their parents, and were discouraged from talking about religious subjects at home. [16]

Joe Reister, staff correspondent for the Courier-Journal related the following testimonies.

40

'I came from an un-Christian home and I had to find Christ on my own. I found Him here at Asbury and now I'm convinced that God is far above everything else.'

'I wish my dear mother were here. I love the Lord with all my heart,' Mike Jordan, student from Hattiesburg, Mississippi. Jordan later told a photographer for the Courier-Journal, who made his picture while he was testifying: 'That flash bulb popping reminded me of the light that has poured into my soul during this revival.'

Many of the students admit they are almost ready to drop from physical exhaustion. But they said they were still spiritually strong.

'I'm awfully tired, physically,' one co-ed sighed, 'but I'm not the least bit tired spiritually.'

An 80-year-old man told of finding God anew.

The testimonies of many participants were almost inaudible at times when the group shouted affirmations.

Another student stood and spoke distinctly. 'I praise the Lord this afternoon for what He means to me,' he said 'If I've ever stood in the way of any of you here, please forgive me.'

Six women students entered the auditorium and seated themselves near the back. Dr. Kenyon pointed them out and said: 'We'll start taking your testimonies right down the line.' All six testified. (Incidently, they had prayed in their rooms that if the Lord wanted them to witness for Him, they would if given a chance. Their chance was given as soon as they entered the building and were seated).

Another six young women walked to the stage and sang their testimonies as a sextet, their voices blending in these words: 'Nobody compares with Jesus. No one so near; no one so dear as He. Jesus alone can take my sadness and give me a wonderful peace.' Some women participants broke into tears at the end of their declarations, but all were firm in their recited convictions. [17]

The singing during the meetings was a fitting compliment to the prevailing spirit of the revival.

Especially during the early stages of this meeting the singing was spontaneous and thrilling. It was a marvellous sight to see hundreds of hands spontaneously and sincerely raised in personal affirmation as the great hymns of the church were sung. Little attention was given to the lighter religious songs. "Amazing Grace" was sung more than any other hymn. The writer noted that during one two-hour period this hymn was spontaneously repeated four times. Other hymns that were sung over and over were "There is a Fountain Filled With Blood" and "What Can Wash Away My Sin?"

The use of the great hymns was one of the indications that this was not just a religious pep meeting. It did not resemble an enthusiastic get-gether wherein zealous collegians cheered "Hurrah for Jesus."[18]

Fanaticism is always a danger in this type of revival. Some who were not present might judge from reports that the meetings were too emotional. However, those who attended these services and saw the leadership of the Holy Spirit will affirm that there was order at all times. There were many "Amens" and "Hallelujahs" when the testimonies were given. At times there was shouting, but this blended into the service and often was hardly noticed. There was liberty in the Spirit!

John Gibson, reporter for the Courier-Journal described it this way:

Voices of the hundreds gathered in the 1,200-seat auditorium resounded throughout the chapel and drifted through open windows as hymns were sung. Most of the seats were occupied and many persons were standing at the rear of the chapel. The hundreds rose to their feet, stretching their arms toward the heavens, as one song followed another. Many left their chapel seats to pray at the altar, so crowded that others knelt and buried their heads in their hands at the front row of seats.

The display of religious fervor, orderly at all times, was spontaneous. Dr. J. B. Kenyon, dean of the school, termed the movement the 'most genuine revival the school has had in some time.' 'We have no apologies to make,' Kenyon said over the loudspeaking system. 'We have found our God anew!' A murmur of assent arose from the lips of the gathered worshippers to greet this statement.

'We may, at times, make a lot of noise,' the dean continued, but don't let that bother you. I've heard a lot more noise at a ball game when the batter strikes out. And isn't this the biggest home run of them all?' 'I've been asked when this will stop. I have only this to say that as long as the Spirit moves you, we have no intention of halting your testimonies.'[19]

There are certain facts about the revival that were never realized by many of those who were present each service. Although the atmosphere was close to heavenly, from time to time there arose problems and situations that threatened to hinder and even halt the revival.

From a human standpoint the revival came at a most inconvenient time. The stage in Hughes Auditorium was set up with curtains hanging ready for a dress rehearsal scheduled for Thursday night - the day the revival began. The praying and testimonies continued throughout the day and increased in momentum as the time for the rehearsal came nearer. Those in charge of producing the play knew people would travel many miles to see it. At the same time it was felt that continuing with it as planned would be detrimental to the revival, and quench the Spirit. Finally, it was decided that the play should be postponed indefinitely.

Then came the problem of unexpected publicity. When those in charge heard about the news items, they wondered whether the news would help or hinder the revival. They feared the publicity would be detrimental if given inaccurately, but felt it would help if given in a true perspective. They did not want to take the risk.

However, newsmen were there the very first night and their cameras flashed intermittenly throughout the service; but such was the Divine Presence that no one seemed to notice them. The Louisville and Lexington papers gave the news release, which spread rapidly throughout the nation.

There was much publicity given on the radio and portions were televised. For a number of days it ranked second as a news feature to the steel strike which was threatening at that time.

On February 26, eight persons, representing the United Press, the Associated Press, and NBC Television, came on the campus and remained for eight hours. The manager of radio station WVLK of Versailles, Kentucky, called and asked the privilege of broadcasting the service over his station.

Again the Holy Spirit undertook. Dean Kenyon had nothing but praise for the newsmen and the excellent way in which they presented their stories to the public.

Along with the activities of the revival, there was the responsibility of maintaining normal operation of the college. While Dr. Z. T. Johnson, Asbury's president, was at the Lakeland Camp Meeting in Florida, Dean J. B. Kenyon contacted him each day, trying to relate to him the occurances on the campus and seeking to be advised by the president. Dr. Johnson was of the opinion that the revival should go on and each day he encouraged Dean Kenyon to carry on as long as the Spirit continued to lead in the service.

Many phone calls came to the office of the dean. Letters came from all over the country, from Massachusetts to Hollywood. Writers gave thanks to God for his visitation, and requested prayer for revivals in their churches. Many asked for gospel teams to come and assist in meetings.

God gave unusual wisdom to the administrative officers and faculty members of the institution in dealing with the problems that arose. Difficulties were swept aside as the eternal concerns of deathless souls and genuine revival took precedence. God was glorified, Christ exalted, and the Holy Spirit was given right of way.

VIII

EVALUATION

It is impossible to adequately evaluate the impact of such a movement as the Asbury revival. Genuine Christianity is always productive and continues to multiply and extend its influence throughout
the ends of the earth. When one ponders for a moment the single
fact that seven to eight hundred volunteers for full time work in the
church are on the campuses of Asbury College and Seminary, the
total influence of a genuine spiritual revival at this strategic center
is staggering to the imagination.

Every sane observer would be frank to admit that there was seed
in this awakening, as in every other revival of history, that
fell by the wayside. Some seed fell on rocky ground. It resulted in
shallow experiences that withered under the heat of worldly re-
sistance. Other seed fell on thorny ground, and in the years that
have passed, the cares of this world, the deceitfulness of riches and
lusts of other things entering in have choked the word. But even in
the face of the tragic reality of spiritual mortality, one would be
foolish indeed if one failed to rejoice in that vast harvest of genuine
and productive Christian life that was reaped, and is still being
reaped, and will be reaped till Jesus comes as a result of those
days.

At the height of its intensity, several students were requested to
record their impressions of the revival for a special edition of the
Collegian. Some of these testimonies are recorded here.

Betty Wheatley, (Freshman) I definitely believe the revival
started because of the prayers of the many groups and the
petitions of many students in their devotions. The one special
thing God did for me was to cause me to trust Him more and
to wait on Him. He also caused me to feel more deeply the
need of prayer.

Judy Kuhn, (Junior) Like everyone else I think the revival
definitely came from prayer and was sent of God. Although
I haven't had any over-whelming feeling, I have learned to
trust the Lord far more than I ever realized was possible.
I know now what living by faith means. "He knoweth the way

that I take and when He hath tried me I shall come forth as gold." (Job 23:10).

Rose Whitehead, (Freshman) Truly I think the revival started by prayer. I have never been so blessed in my life as I have during this revival. Some people have made decisions now which will affect their whole lives and the world too. I thank the Lord that I am privileged to be at Asbury during this revival and feel that I have grown closer to Him.

Roberto Lenz, Cuba, (Sophomore) I think that by the power of God, prayers of students and professors of this institution this revival started. This has been a time of great spiritual refreshing for me. It is beyond me to express how I feel deeply in my heart. I praise the Lord everyday for having led me to Asbury, for I have received such a blessing, not only because of the good education, but also because of the good spiritual atmosphere. I love the Lord with all my heart, and my goal in life is to serve Him in my own country. Praise to His name for the revival.

Eldon Raymond, (Freshman) I think definitely this revival was of God. My name for it is 'spontaneous combustion.' God worked everything up to a head and let it blow. I think it was definitely because of prayer. God has been wanting to give it to us for a long time. My prayer is that it will continue until every person on Asbury's campus will know Christ in His saving and sanctifying power. I believe this revival and the publicity it was given by the papers and over the television has been God's own way of reaching souls that might never have been reached otherwise. I thank God that He has shown me more the need of prayer and also thank Him for being able to preach a gospel that can be lived. [20]

The reactions of reporters from secular press is especially significant as it represents the more objective opinion of the detached observer.

Edwin Leavens, editor of Lexington's Community News, made a trip to Wilmore when he learned of the revival and the following summary of his impressions was published in his paper:

I don't know if the trip was made out of curiosity, willingness to see this thing for myself, or to try to find an explanation for it.

Saturday afternoon, accompanied by photographer Harold

Rogers, I made the trip to the college. As we approached the campus, it appeared deserted. No activity of any kind was noticeable. When we entered the grounds of the college the sounds of singing could be heard. Pulling up in front of one of the buildings, we inquired if the revival was still in progress. A young man replied, "Yes, praise the Lord, it is." The expression was made with such obvious and deep sincerity it took me by surprise.

We climbed the stairs to Hughes Auditorium, the scene of the revival. It was already in the third day. As we entered the building there could be seen a cluster of young people gathered about the front center portion of the meeting hall.

Not being accustomed to the surroundings or the activities, Rogers and I decided to sit in the rear of the auditorium. For approximately twenty minutes we sat there watching as the students gave vent to their beliefs.

I have never seen such happy people. An observer could not help but notice the youthfulness of the gathering. There was much singing of hymns, prayers, testimonials, and confessions. Periodically, some of the students would mount the platform to give public testimony, or to affirm their faith in God. To be impressed by such scenes the revival had to be witnessed.

Soon we were approached by one of the students of the college. He asked us if we would care to take part in the ceremonies being conducted. Hesitatingly, Rogers and I told him we were there to find the reason for this marathon religious demonstration to God. Never witnessing anything like it before, we wanted to see how it was being conducted.

For close to an hour this young man, a native of New York State, told us of his finding God. He related his story with such obvious sincerity one couldn't help but be struck by it. His faith in God was a wonder to behold. Here was a young man in the material world of today apparently oblivious to it all. He seemed not bothered or worried about such things that appear to be the major problems of the young.

During our talk the revival continued at its spirited pace. People kept coming into the auditorium and joining in the singing and praying.

It had been our intention to remain there approximately 15 minutes, get a story, perhaps a picture or two, then leave. But it proved so appealing to stay there and watch this almost unbelievable demonstration of religion, we stayed for a much longer period of time.

As for the young fellow we talked with, I have never seen anyone so happy. He gave the appearance of actually glowing with happiness. A warmth that you wished could be catching. Here was a sight to put envy into the heart of anyone.

He told us how the revival had started. One of the students, Barefoot by name, had offered a testimonial during one of the religious meetings held regularly during the school period. From there the spirit of the movement was reflected throughout the student body, and the revival began.

Throughout the talk the Asbury student conversing with Rogers and me kept repeating his convictions. It was his goal to go out into the missionary field and preach. For the better part of our talk he tried to tell us of his feelings. Words apparently could not do the task. All one had to do was to look at this student and become convinced that he had found something to alter the course of his life.

Patiently and carefully he told us of his conversion. He explained his attitude prior to receiving his beliefs. Cynicism and disbelief had been his chief fortes when he enrolled in Asbury College. The firm religious beliefs of his fellow-students made him give long thought to the idea of a good and loving God. Friday, the second day of the movement, he said his faith became firm, unwavering, and permanent. When he found his faith, he said nothing else mattered.

Youth was the mainstay of the whole movement. Although there were a few older people scattered throughout the gathering, it was very obvious that it was predominately the students of the college who were the main participants.

Fanaticism had no part in it. There were no great emotional or theatrical displays. Those who got up in the front of the microphone gave vent to their beliefs. Sympathy and understanding of the audience was always with them. It was one of the most moving experiences I have ever witnessed.

Reflecting, the thought occurred to me that perhaps more of this is the answer to the war-racked world. When youth returns to God, it is hard to see how militarists can convince them that war is so necessary.

Whatever the answer, the most obvious thing gleaned from this religious movement at Asbury College is that it beats an armament race anytime. [21] (Incidently, Herbie Van Vorce was the student interviewed by this editor).

One year after the revival, newsman George Reynolds of the Lexington Herald returned to the campus in hopes that there might be a recurrence. He wrote:

Students and faculty members of Asbury College today had happy but solemn memories of the great spontaneous revival which started on their campus a year ago and continued for five days and nights.

Everyone was aware of the anniversary today, but there was no movement to rekindle the dramatic demonstrations of religious zeal which last year gained nation-wide interest and brought hundreds of people here to testify of their renewed faith in God.

The sunshine-brightened campus was quiet today, with students walking to and from classes and several small boys playing ball on the front lawn. Two students strolled from a building with their parents, showing them the sights. Occasional laughter burst from open windows of classrooms.

At Hughes Memorial Auditorium where a student arose during chapel exercises last February 23 and asked to testify, launching the greatest revival in the school's history, two care-takers cleaned and adjusted seats in preparation for tonight's showing of a junior class play.

Dean Kenyon emphasized today that nobody expected a renewal of the revival on its anniversary, because it was not an organized service, and participants had no intention of creating an annual observance.

The now-famous revival rapidly grew in intensity and size after it began at Thursday-morning chapel services. By Saturday, it had become nation-wide in interest, and reporters, photographers and radio-television personnel flocked to the auditorium to describe the activities.

Students were reminded of the revival's anniversary at chapel exercises yesterday, but all of them seemed to realize that such a movement could not recur on schedule.

Betty Brown, a student from Nashville, Tennessee, best explained their attitude. 'We could try again and again,' she said, 'but it would never be the same.'[22]

Faculty members of Asbury College were perhaps best qualified to give a mature and realistic evaluation of the revival. Dr. W. W. Holland, chairman of the Division of Philosophy and Religion made the following observations:

If I were required to express the most significant thing about that great spiritual movement, I should say it was the genuine sincerity on the part of all who participated.

The revival was not planned by man or the college; it was not brought about by organization, any great evangelist or any outstanding human personality or personalities. It came in my judgment, as the result of the sincere prayers of the faculty, officers, and the student body. It was not promoted by any great preaching.

No effort was made on the part of the faculty or of the administration to superimpose the revival spirit upon the student body. We wanted only the will and the work of God.

For several weeks the prayer life of Asbury College had been deepening. Groups of students had assembled for fasting and prayer with the faith and expectation that 'If my people which are called by my name shall humble themselves, and pray, and seek my face, and turn from their wicked ways; then will I hear from heaven, and will forgive their sins, and will heal their land.' (II Chronicles 7:14)[23]

Marvin Dean, Glee Club Director:

I shall forever praise the Lord for what this revival at Asbury has meant to the student body, the faculty, the community, and the nation. My prayer is that the revival fires will continue to sweep this nation and the world, for the salvation of men is our only hope from total destruction. This was a time of heart-searching in my own life, and how I praise Him for meeting my need. As director of the glee club, I am so grateful that we are all in one accord as never before; and I believe that God will use us in a mighty way as we go out to witness for Him.

Leon Fisher, Psychology Department:

One of the most significant things in this revival has been the reality of God's presence. Many times religion is merely a projection of the imagination - without reality. God is His own evidence - and this has given us an experience we can know is real.

Virginia Hayes, Language Department:

This revival is the moving of the Holy Spirit upon our hearts to bring us to the realization that God has a way out of this world of confusion if we will commit ourselves to His leadership.

Dr. D. C. Corbitt, Chairman of History Department:

The attention of the whole nation has been drawn to Asbury by this revival. 'For unto whomsoever much is given, of him shall much be required; and to whom men have committed much, of him they will ask the more.' (Luke 12:48).

Mrs. D. Corbitt, Language Department:

The success of this revival can be measured not so much by its horizontal spread to other places as by the depth to which it has gone in each individual heart.

Dr. A. T. Putney, Chairman of English Department:

In my opinion the present revival is more nearly akin to the experience of the early disciples on that day of Pentecost than I have heard of in modern time. I believe that this revival is God's answer to the crying need of the world and that it has come at an opportune moment in the life of Asbury that the students who are going out will go with lighted torches to kindle revival fires throughout the world. I have been particularly impressed with the spirit of spontaneity which has characterized the revival. Another feature has been the sense of clarity of direction which has come from the Holy Spirit with a minimum of human guidance and instruction.

Dr. Z. T. Johnson, President of Asbury College:

There is no doubt that the outpourings of the Spirit have been genuine and penetrating. This has not been planned or humanly directed. It is not a man-made affair in any sense of the word.
I knew from reports which reached me in Florida by radio, telephone, and newspaper that God had given an unusual visitation. I was told that it was impossible to realize the extent of it without being present. I found this to be true the moment I reached the campus. [24]

The mighty forces of God released during this revival cannot go unnoticed by sincere believers. Serious reflection upon these events should cause us real concern. Surely it is "vivid proof, that the days of revival are not over," and "that the power of God unto salvation is applicable in the middle of the 20th century." [25] Revivals can be had today in God's own way when the conditions are met.

Elements of the apostolic pattern are here displayed in a modern setting. Clearly seen is the need for fervent and intercessory prayer on the part of God's people. Absolute obedience to the revelation of God's will, and utter and complete dependence upon God to effect His own sovereign purpose.

Dr. T. M. Anderson, professor at Asbury College, mightily used of God in meetings following the Asbury revival has observed:

> With these conditions met, we can have a visitation of God. My heart is set against a kind of professional ministry that has just so many sermons to preach and so many songs to sing and a certain program to be rigidly followed. We don't mean to shove the Holy Spirit away, we don't mean to crowd Him out; but we do it nevertheless with a great many of these programs and human plans. We overlook the necessity of absolute and complete dependence on the Holy Spirit.

He concludes that in his opinion there are three things that will aid in bringing mighty visitations of God: that people find a place to pray in the early morning, that those knowing there is more for them in the grace of God respond promptly to the Spirit, and that churches desist from too many programs and too much ritual and give God a chance to use earnest prayer and simple messages to manifest His power.

This meeting and others like it challenge us to search our own hearts and see why God cannot give us revival again. But more, it inspires our hope and encourages our faith to actually expect revival in our day. Indeed, it makes us aware that God is on the throne, that He is able to supply all our needs, and that it is His desire to give the Holy Spirit to His children.

IX

SEQUEL

Revival is not an unpredictable, mysterious phenomenon. It is God's response to heart honesty, contrite repentance, and desperate, prevailing intercession. In March of 1958 God sent another genuine and spontaneous revival to the campus of Asbury College. Although it did not receive the nationwide attention of the previous awakening, in many respects it was remarkably similar. The earnest intercession, the brokeness of spirit, honesty with God and man, the marathon of hearts seeking the Lord and the radiant testimonies of fresh won victories - all were reminiscent of that mighty deluge of heaven-sent blessing that fell upon the campus in 1950. God could do it again and did do it again when His people were willing to pay the price.

On March 1, 1958, the regular chapel service began at 8:00 a.m. and progressed as usual. Mr. Leon Fisher, professor of Psycology, was the speaker of the hour. He preached a powerful and searching message on "Soul Sickness", from the text, (II Corinthians 13:5), "Examine yourselves, whether ye be in the faith; prove your own selves."

As he continued one could sense that the Holy Spirit was in charge, so much so, that when the message was being brought to its conclusion there was a mighty sense of the presence of God in the midst of the people. Just as professor Fisher was about to close the service, Arthur Osborne, a Junior and former class president, came to the platform and asked to say a word. He began to pour out his heart in confession. He said he would have been a better class president had he been right with the Lord. He asked the students to forgive him for setting a poor example of Christian living. As he started for the altar, he invited campus leaders and others who had slipped away from the Lord to join him in confession and repentance. The Spirit of God used that simple, honest statement to drive the sword of conviction deep into hearts. About seventy-five students responded almost immediately.

No sooner did they pray through to assurance than they stepped to the platform and testified to what God had done. Before long forty or more students were waiting in line to stand before the pulpit microphone and witness to the saving, sanctifying and reclaiming grace of God.

As the meeting progressed choruses were sung at intervals and prayer was offered from time to time. As the witnessing continued, many confessed laxities in their Christian lives. Confessions were made to professors and to the administration of the college because of criticisms which were made previous to the revival.

One could see that this revival needed no preacher. The whole atmosphere was charged with the presence of God already. In fact, preaching would have been out of place here, so mighty was the presence of the Holy One. As one student expressed it, "Anyone who came under the powerful influence of this indescribable, but powerful visitation of the Holy Spirit, would from then on have an extra responsibility in his Christian faith." It was not a time of demonstration or great outward excitement, but more of a deep, refining, quiet as the Holy Spirit was searching hearts and bringing pungent conviction, breaking down stubborn wills and melting hardened hearts. "It was as if all the windows were opened wide as in springtime, and the soft zephyrs of fresh air swept through to clear the atmosphere and make it clean and pure. The air was stirred and all the lurking pollution seemed to be brought to light and cleansed."[26]

In a movement such as this even though there is little need of human effort or preaching, it seems that God lays on the hearts of some individuals to give guidance to the services, that is, to keep the congregation in the spirit of prayer and supplication and at the same time keep the meeting under control.

For this needed leadership, Dr. Clarence V. Hunter and professor Robert F. Wiley, faculty members at Asbury College, seemed to have been chosen of the Lord. Together they spent numerous hours, day and night, in the auditorium dealing with those about the altar, praying, leading in the hymns and choruses, and guiding the testimonies. Both men were equipped by the Spirit with unusual perception and wisdom. Consistently, they kept the great crowd's attention centered on the glory of God. "Praise God!" "Give God the Glory, brother!" "God is faithful," they would urge. They carried an intense burden for the revival and the Lord blessed their willing efforts.

Many students and faculty members sensed a vital need of a spiritual resurgence. At the preceding Thursday noon fast prayer meeting, the leader, John Morris, student body president, asked the question, "What would you like to see take place at Asbury?" Many persons present, students and faculty alike, expressed that they would like to see a sweeping revival on the campus.

This same deep feeling was expressed in the faculty prayer meeting on Friday, the day before God manifested Himself in the chapel service. Also, on this same day, there were groups of young people meeting in their rooms waiting before God in prayer. With faith and expectation, they looked to the Lord for an unusual manifestation of His power.

Urgent intercession at the college and among the church people and expectant appropriation by faith brought divine response. Hundreds of students and townspeople were brought from darkness to light, and received the forgiveness of sins and an inheritance among them that are sanctified by faith.

The marathon of intercession, repentance and testimony continued unbroken from 8:00 a.m. on Saturday until about 11:00 p.m. on Monday. Throughout the rest of the week regular revival meetings were scheduled at the Methodist Church with Dr. T. M. Anderson as evangelist.

The most prominent feature of the revival was the testimonies. The common denominator of these testimonies was love - love for God, and love for one another. It was out of hearts overflowing with love, that many confessions were made relating to adjustments with God and other people. These confessions related to pride, selfishness, unholy ambitions and the like. Expressed in the various testimonies was the desire to do the whole will of God. It was evident that under the scrutinizing searchings of the Holy Spirit those who testified had been brought face to face with God, concerning His will for their lives.

On Saturday night the Asbury College Concert Band was scheduled to present a concert. Although there had been extensive publicity coverage of the concert, and groups were expected from distant towns, the director, Paul Rader, deemed it advisable to postpone the program. The regularly planned services at the Wilmore Methodist Church were abandoned. A temperance speaker who was to have the morning service, being anxious that the Holy Spirit lead, consented to come again. After another refreshing service on Sunday morning, Dr. Robert L. Anderson the pastor announced a meeting in Hughes Auditorium for that afternoon. It too was a precious meeting, the altar lined again and again with seekers. Students radiant with victory in Christ gave thrilling testimonies. While a group continued to pray in the auditorium, others attended the regular Sunday night service at the Methodist Church. Once again the Holy Spirit blanketed the audience and many were swept into the high tide of spiritual power. Local high school students wept openly as they came before the audience to witness, without fear, to what God had done for them.

Following the church service on Sunday night, the revival burst forth anew in Hughes Auditorium, where an intercessory vigil of prayer had been maintained. Some five hundred persons gathered without previous announcement. This was the crowning service of the revival. The evening was filled with great and thrilling spiritual experiences. It was a mountain-top of Holy Ghost blessing that was transforming in its impact.

About 10:00 p.m. a Chinese student, Joseph Yong, stepped to the microphone. He testified concerning his conversion and the gracious evidences of God's hand in his life. Then amid shouts of praise, he voiced that great song of testimony, "It Took A Miracle." After he had finished and left the platform, an ex-G.I. stood up and said:

As I sat there in my seat, God asked me whether I could love this man (obviously referring to the Chinese student who had appeared just before him.) Could I love him as I love others? I was in a prison camp for some weeks and we were treated with much cruelty. I have seen my buddies slaughtered and persecuted. I had nothing but hatred for these people. When I passed them on the campus my stomach seemed to turn upside down. I would snub them. But the love of Christ has taken that all away. Thank God, that hatred is all gone. I have no ill-feeling toward them, and want them to forgive me for my feelings. God has forgiven me and I want them to.

Joseph Yong shouted with joy, and the power of God fell in fresh anointing on the service.

Grace and Ruth Davis, sisters at Asbury, were powerfully used of God singing in evangelistic services after the revival began to spread. That night after bringing a bright and clear witness to the sanctifying power of the Spirit, they lifted their voices together under the powerful blessing of the Holy Ghost and sang "Glory to Jesus". The power of God came upon the audience in such a manner, that the majority of those present were either laughing, weeping or shouting with sheer joy.

Many unsaved and backslidden students were kept awake all that night by the conviction of the Spirit. About midnight, an influential and brilliant student for whom many had been praying entered the auditorium and took a seat near the back. A great volume of prayer went up for his conversion as students gathered about the altar to intercede. Others went back to encourage him to surrender his life to Christ. At about 2:00 a.m. he stood to his feet, strode resolutely to the front and threw himself down at the altar. A glorious shout of victory went up from those who were interceding that sent a thrilling shock through every heart present. God had mightily answered prayer.

On Monday evening, Dr. Z. T. Johnson took charge of the service. About 11:00 p. m. he announced that he thought it advisable to dismiss the public service. He encouraged students to rest and then to continue seeking the mind of the Lord in private. Services were announced for the following night at the Methodist Church. Prayer meetings continued at intervals all week at the college. Lights burned in the auditorium each night and individuals continued to seek God. At the same time services were continued at the Methodist Church under the preaching of Dr. T. M. Anderson, who had returned from his labors in the evangelistic field. The Lord continued to bless during these services and hundreds received help at the altar. On Monday night there were from 500 to 700 present and on Tuesday about 300 were in attendance. The attendance jumped to 600 on Wednesday as compared to the regular attendance of 100. About twenty persons sought the Lord on Wednesday.

After this weekend of victory at Asbury, ministerial students in both the college and seminary began to return from their pastorates, reporting gracious outpourings of the Holy Spirit upon their services. In one instance a student went to a church on Sunday morning and merely told the people what was taking place at Asbury and thirty-seven out of the congregation of forty-four prayed through to victory about the altar.

The Wells Memorial Methodist Church in Jackson, Mississippi, again was caught up in the spirit of revival. Rev. Hollis T. Landrum, pastor of the church, was leading the regular Wednesday evening prayer service when the people began to testify and confess their heart needs. Revival took hold. The testimonies which started that evening continued in number and spirit. This unusual revival lasted twenty-one days. Rev. Marvin Osbourne and the pastor led the services each night, which were completely unplanned. Many churches in and around Jackson began to call Wells Church for workers to come and hold revivals. Word had come on the first Wednesday evening that another revival had begun at Asbury. At the request of Rev. Landrum three Asbury students flew to Jackson immediately, their fare being paid by the church. The following weekend, Dr. and Mrs. Clarence V. Hunter and six Asbury girls went to Jackson in a station wagon, witnessing as they traveled. Also, four boys from the college and one from the seminary drove the same weekend to help in the Jackson revival.

From the Wells church a revival began on Sunday, March 16 at the Epworth Methodist Church, where Rev. Osbourne assisted the pastor, Rev. Hillman Wolfe, in the morning service. Rev. Wolfe said:

Rev. Osbourne did not preach what one would call a sermon at this service, he merely commented very briefly, then gave a simple invitation for all who felt in their heart that they needed to seek forgiveness from God and from one another to do so by coming forward. The altar was filled very quickly and about three-fourths of the entire congregation was on their knees before God before the service closed. A similar service was held that night with about the same response from people who were not there in the morning service.

Many churches in Jackson experienced a revival which was not planned and had no preaching. No particular pattern was followed. The services were informal and ran into the night with no set hour for stopping. Among the churches which reported such a movement were Antioch Methodist Church, Foxworth-Hopewell Methodist Churches and Laurel Methodist Church.

Under the direction of Rev. Osbourne a television program called "Revival of Prayer" was originated over WJTV in Jackson. Many letters poured in requesting prayer and assuring prayer support for the most unusual revival which had come to Jackson. It was estimated that during the first three weeks of this revival approximately 1000 people had been to the altars.

In Nashville, Tennessee, Asburians visited Travecca Nazarene College and witnessed in a chapel service where spontaneous altar services were seen. Including the results of other services held in that area, approximately sixty decisions were made.

During a one week revival at the West Huron Methodist Church at Fort Austin, Michigan, about forty accepted Christ and foundations were laid for the formation of Bible clubs in two different high schools.

In Milwaukee, Wisconsin, seven Asburians witnessed forty victories at the local Salvation Army Corps. A visit to the Men's Social Service Center resulted in four victories.

At Freeport, Illinois, in a Free Methodist Church twenty-five persons took a stand for Christ in a service led by Asbury students.

Spartansburg, South Carolina, saw a four-day revival, led by four Asburians, who reported twenty-five persons converted.

Asburians were faced with a lack of enthusiasm at Atlantic, Pennsylvania, but six souls were saved in the first such movement in that church for years. Revival kindlings were started and were burning as the students returned to Asbury.

The Methodist Church in Mt. Zion, Ohio saw nineteen persons kneel at the altar and a stirring among leaders of nearby churches.

Excellent attendance and twenty-five victories were reported from the Bethesada Methodist Church in Indiana. Four Salvationists conducted a ten-day tour of eleven Salvation Army Corps in the Indiana division. Over fifty meetings which included open airs, visiting hospitals, high schools, civic clubs and radio programs were conducted and 101 victories were reported.

It would be hard to estimate how many people were saved because of this awakening. As in the case of the former Asbury revival proper evaluation must await the revelation of the record in the Lamb's Book of Life.

God's formula for revival is still the same. If His people will seek His face in travailing and prevailing prayer and will lay bare their hearts before Him in honest confession and repentance; if they will commit their wills to obedience at any cost, revival is inevitable.

Behold, the Lord's hand is not shortened, that it cannot save; neither his ear heavy, that it cannot hear: but your iniquites have separated between you and your God, and your sins have hid his face from you, that he will not hear. (Isaiah 59:1, 2)

If my people, which are called by my name, shall humble themselves, and pray, and seek my face, and turn from their wicked ways; then will I hear from heaven, and will forgive their sin, and will heal their land. (II Chronicles 7:14)

As the Saviour tarries, may God grant to send upon the world a mighty conflagration of revival fire through the power of the Holy Spirit until every knee shall bow and every tongue confess that Jesus Christ is Lord to the glory of God the Father.

FOOTNOTES

1. Contained in a letter written by Rev. Dee Cobb in November, 1956.
2. William W. Holland, "The Asbury College Revival," *The Pentecostal Herald*, I, No. 44 (March 15), The Herald Press: Louisville, Ky., 1950, p. 4.
3. *Ibid.*
4. *The Asbury Collegian* (Revival Edition), XXXIII, No. 18, (March, 1950), Wilmore, Ky., p. 4.
5. W. Curry Mavis, "Revival Tides Are Rising," *The Christian Minister*, (April, 1950), II, No. 1, Light and Life Press: Winona Lake, Ind., p. 1.
6. The Asbury Collegian, *op. cit.*, p. 1.
7. *Dallas Morning News* (Associated Press), "College Revival Turns Marathon" (February 25, 1950).
8. Jack Lewyn (reporter), "Revival at Asbury Continues Into Fifth Day," *The Lexington Herald* (February 27, 1950), Lexington, Ky., p. 1.
9. Holland, *op. cit.*, p. 13.
10. T. M. Anderson, *Prevailing Prayer* (Fourth Edition), Wilmore Press: Wilmore, Ky., 1951, pp. 34 36.
11. The Asbury Collegian, *op. cit.*, p. 4.
12. *Ibid.*, p. 3.
13. Contained in a letter written by Rev. R. E. Case in November, 1956.
14. *The Asbury Collegian*, op. cit., p. 3.
15. Mavis, *op. cit.*, p. 1.
16. Jack Lewyn (reporter), "Asbury Student Fervor Continues Strong," *The Herald Leader*, Lexington, Ky. (February 25), 1950.
17. Joe Reister (Staff Correspondent), "Asbury Revival Likely to go Several Days," *The Courier - Journal*, Louisville, Ky. (February 25, 1950).
18. Mavis, *op. cit.*, p. 2.
19. John Gibson (AP staff writer), "Townspeople and Teachers Join in as Asbury College Revival Continues," IX, No. 56, *The Courier Journal*, Louisville, Ky. (February 24, 1950).
20. The Asbury Collegian, *op. cit.*, p. 2.
21. Edwin T. Leavens, ed., "Impressions of Asbury Revival as Witnessed by Editor, *The Community News - Lexington's Weekly Newspaper*, I, No. 44, Lexington, Ky. (March 3, 1950).
22. George Reynolds (Herald staff writer), "Anniversary of Spontaneous Asbury Revival Noted Quietly by College Student Body," *The Herald*, Lexington, Ky. (February 24, 1951).
23. Holland, *op. cit.*, p. 4.
24. The Asbury Collegian, *op. cit.*, pp. 2-4.
25. Mavis, *op. cit.*, p. 2.
26. J. C. McPheeters, ed., "Refreshing Visitation of the Spirit at Asbury, *The Herald*, LXIV, The Herald Press: Louisville, Ky. (March 26, 1950), p. 9.